D0700345

BEST OF
KITCHEN DESIGN

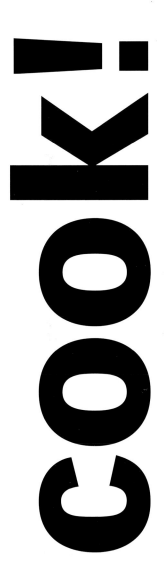

Imprint

The Deutsche Bibliothek is registering this publication in the Deutsche Nationalbibliographie; detailed bibliographical information can be found on the internet at http://dnb.ddb.de

ISBN 978-3-03768-013-1
© 2009 by Braun Publishing AG
www.braun-publishing.ch

1st edition 2009

Project coordinator: Annika Schulz
Editorial staff: Dagmar Glück
Translation: Stephen Roche, Hamburg
Graphic concept: Michaela Prinz

BEST OF
KITCHEN DESIGN

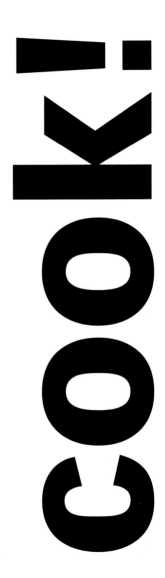

BRAUN

Preface

As an architectural form the kitchen reflects social structures and cultural revolutions. It is in a process of change. Cooking is no longer a daily-practiced craft, but rather an art form that is becoming rarer. This trend is reflected in modern cuisine. The following collection presents projects whose language of form expresses the both the culinary traditions of various countries and the individual design preferences of homeowners. At the same time, certain trends such as clarity and openness are recognizable across all continents.

The culture of food in industrialized nations has been transformed in recent decades. It is becoming rarer for families to gather around a table for a self-prepared meal. People lack time, and as a result cooking has been 'outsourced'. More and more convenience products have come on the market. We feed ourselves from plastic containers and frozen food, or eat out in restaurants. But our leave-taking from one of humanity's oldest cultural skills is neither straightforward nor total. This is proven by a current trend in the opposite direction: at weekends or evenings cooking with friends is being celebrated as a kind of 'happening'. As time for cooking becomes scarcer the theme of cooking is becoming more prominent. The market for cookery books is booming, cooking courses for all target groups are more popular than ever, and the army of TV cooks grows ever larger. 'Anyone can cook' is the universal message.

This transformation of culinary culture is reflected in the place where cooking takes place (or not, as the case may be),

and thus the kitchen is adjusted to social changes: in our hectic lives the kitchen functions as the family's center of communication. For that reason, architects are integrating the kitchen into the living space and are finding off-beat solutions for fluid transitions between both areas. In a sensual play with surprising combinations of materials, in stunning combinations of light and form, designers are creating kitchens that are prestigious stages for the modern dinner party host. Cooking for family and friends is being celebrated as a social event, and particular attention is being paid to the design of the venue for this event. The dominant materials are stainless steel with glossy varnished or robust wooden surfaces. Front panels of continuous smoked oak, olive or walnut veneer represent the new comfort of the kitchen. Stone sets an additional tone as a natural material.

When the kitchen becomes the meeting point and nerve center of the active family, one single fixture becomes indispensable: the monolithic work unit. As shown in the case of the 'white & stainless steel' kitchen designed by Andreas Hansel Design, an entire extended family can gather around one of these units. The kitchen unit is a stylish reinterpretation of the original kitchen. The earliest known kitchen was discovered in the vicinity of Jericho and dates from the period 8,000 BC. Simple, open-air clay ovens were used communally by several families. The earliest known indoor ovens have been found in Anatolia dating from approximately one millennium later. Up to the late Middle Ages the kitchen was the most important room in a community. With the invention of the fireplace and flue, the oven was moved from the centre of the room to the wall, and lost its place at the center of household life.

The first designer kitchens were created in the Twenties by the Viennese architect Margarete Schütte-Lihotzky. Her Frankfurt Kitchen was designed as a single-person cooking unit, to be operated by the housewife operating in secret. The Frankfurt Kitchen could be adapted to different architectural floor plans. The demonstration kitchen had a rectangular layout with measurements of only 3.44 x 1.87 meters with maximum functionality. It included, for example, a fold-up ironing board, a swivel chair and pull-out shelving. The kitchen was originally designed in deep blue, which, it was claimed, repelled mosquitoes.

Functionality is still an important theme in kitchen design. High-tech appliances and all kinds of integrated utensils make the private designer kitchen into a culinary workshop that holds its own with professional kitchens. All of the profane aids and equipment disappear behind smooth surfaces and handle-less front panels. Because the kitchen is part of the living area and therefore visible to every visitor it is also tidier than ever. Another solution is to conceal the kitchen completely: the 'Green-HAB' kitchen unit, for example, is hidden behind a perforated sliding partition (Kroiz Architecture). Steinert & Bitterling have designed their compact kitchen so that it can, if necessary, be folded away into a decorative and rustic cabinet.

Nowadays, kitchens are no longer designed with mosquitoes in mind. Instead men have become a greater consideration. Ever since cooking became socially acceptable as a male pursuit, there has been a trend towards created the male kitchen. The non-colors black, white and metallic predominate in addition to masculine earth tones and high-gloss surfaces in car-paint colors. The link to auto design is conspicuous in the streamlined design of the kitchen frame in the Birner residence (Marco Glashagen Interior Design), a kind of cockpit for the culinary male.

Every detail of the kitchens included in this book is a declaration of love to the art of cooking and a homage to the creativity of kitchen owners. Life moves through the kitchen, so cook!

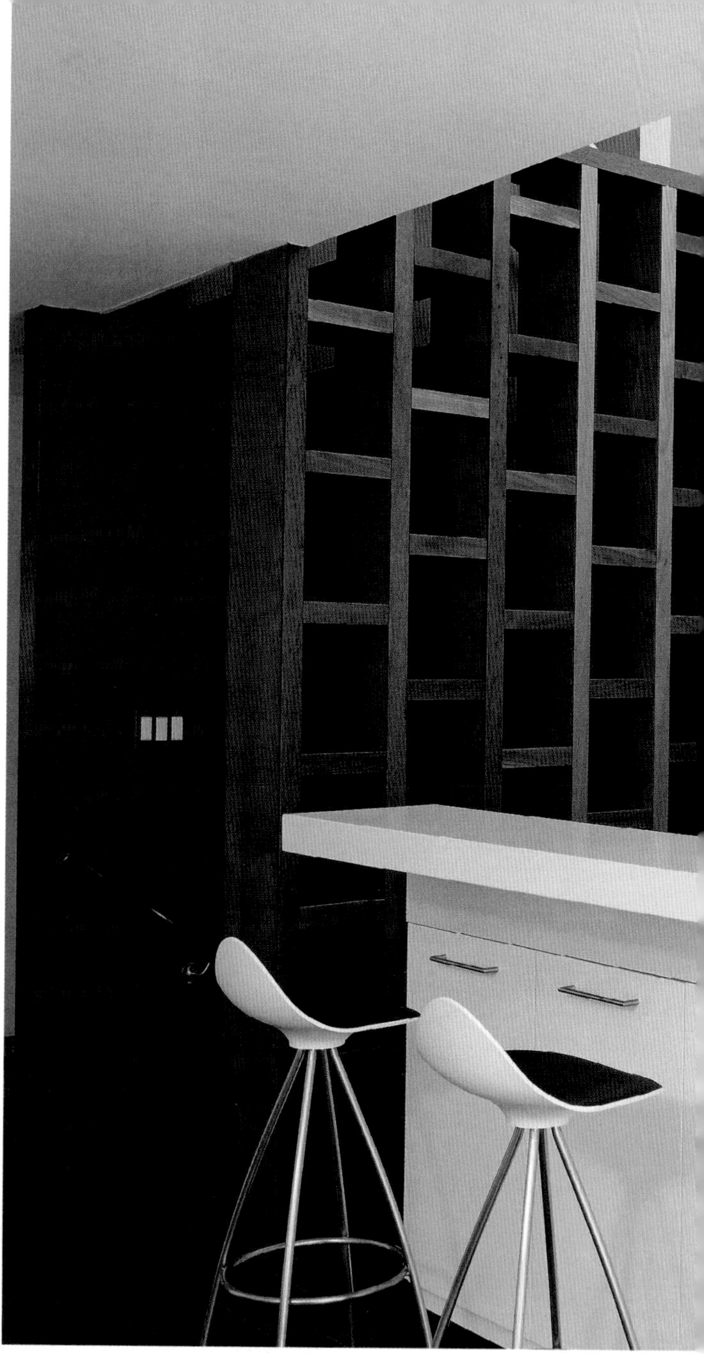

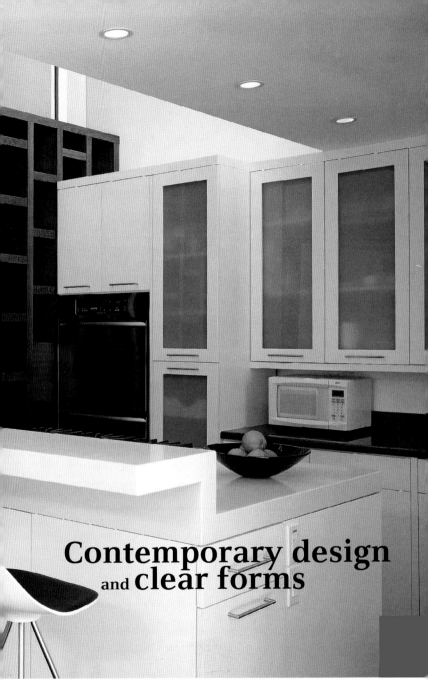

Contemporary design
and clear forms

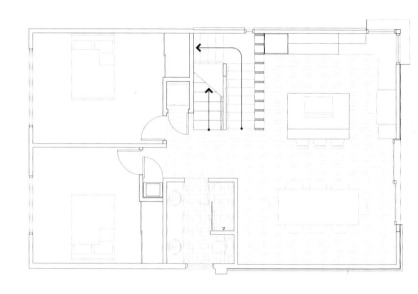

Sleek lines with **warm lighting** create a **compact** yet functional **urban** loft kitchen

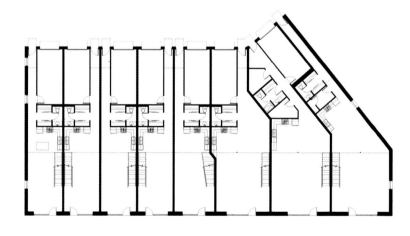

261 Adlon Road Residence | Encino | MAKE Architecture

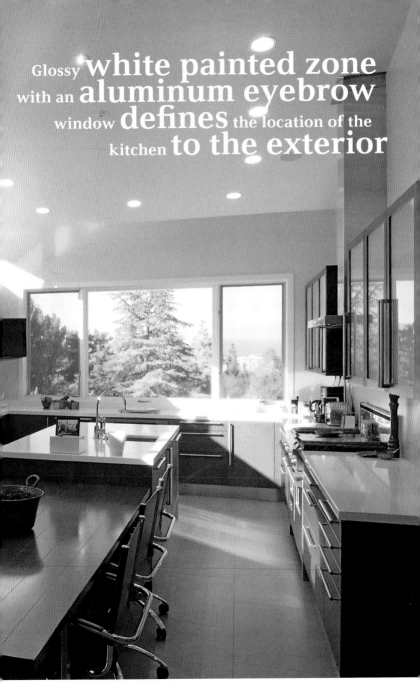

Glossy **white painted zone** with an **aluminum eyebrow** window **defines** the location of the kitchen **to the exterior**

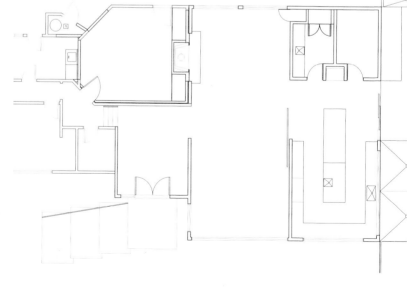

A **family kitchen**
designed for **cooking** and
enjoying food

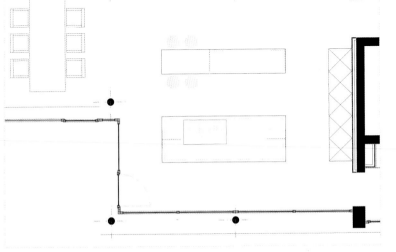

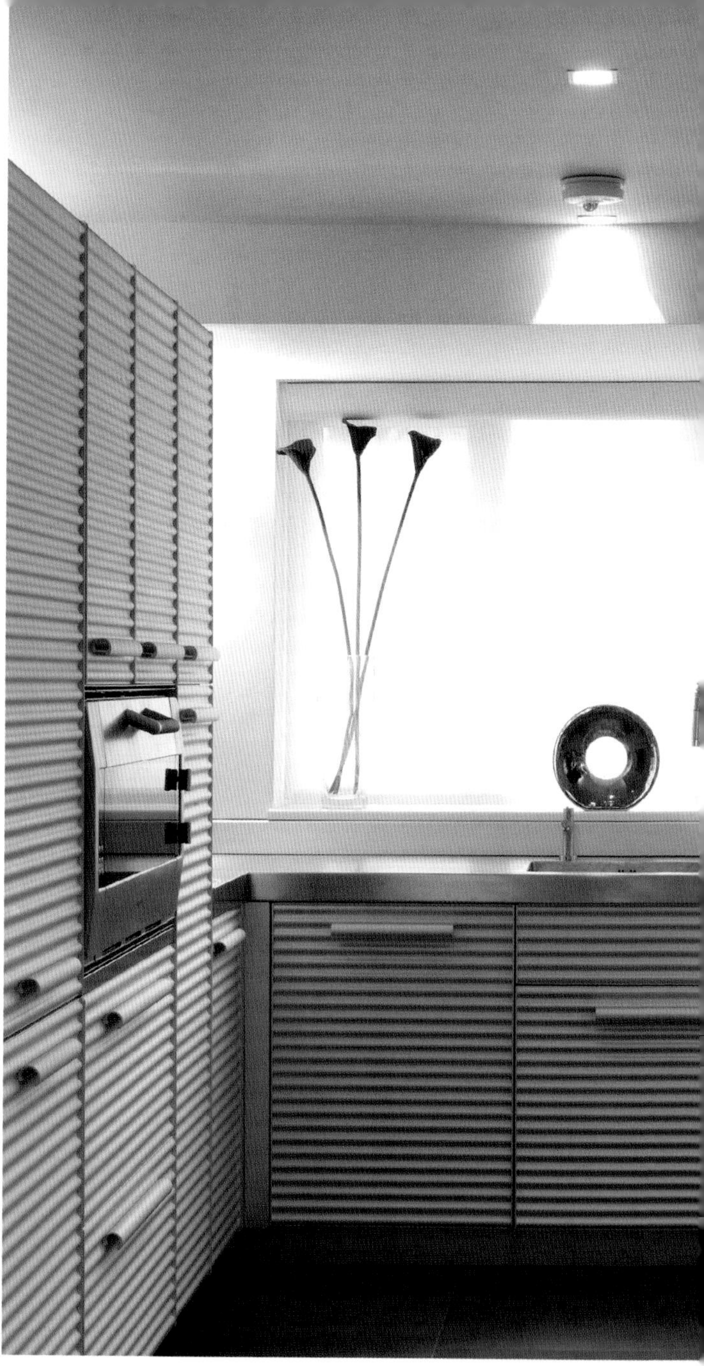

This **compact kitchen** has a **futuristic,** streamlined look that uses **natural aluminum** and **glossy black lacquer**

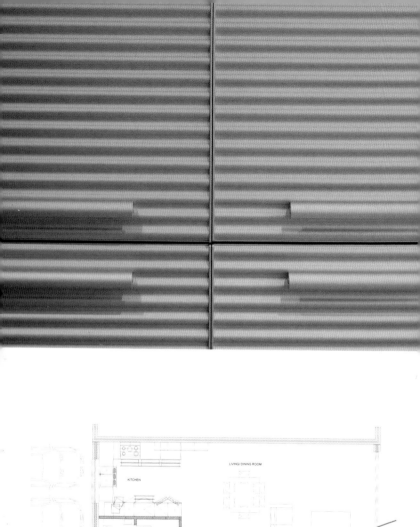

Apartment in Heidelberg | Heidelberg | AAG Loebner Weber, Freie Architekten BDA

Open plan kitchen
with wooden furniture

Atelier House Meier Soglio l Soglio l Ruinelli Associati architetti

More space
for family living

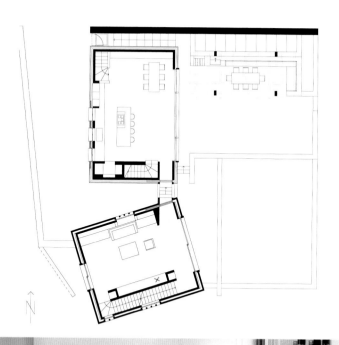

The **floor** covering in **split Norwegian slate** blen— **harmoniously** with the **calm white** surfaces

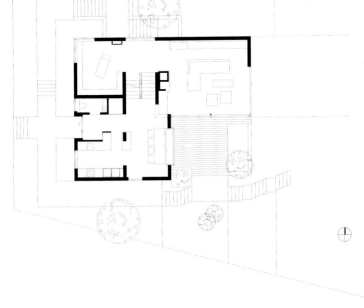

Bath Kitchen l Bath l Johnny Grey Studios

A family kitchen designed to combine an inviting working area with a comfortable living space

The interior is a **restrained palette** of **crisp white walls** playing off **limeston** floors, natural wood, **and ste**

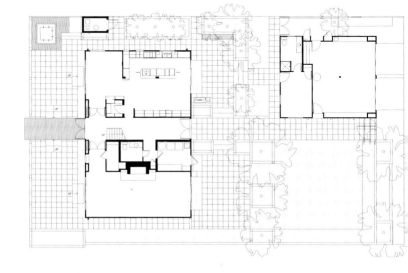

Birner Residence | Nuremberg | marco glashagen innenarchitektur

The **special feature** of this kitchen is a **free-floating ten-meter-long** sideboard whose design is reminiscent of **an** aircraft

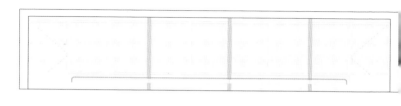

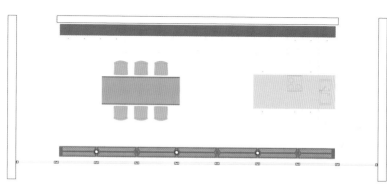

861 **Cabbagetown Residence** | Toronto | Dubbeldam Design Architects

A compact, **functional kitchen** that is sleek, **modern** and designed **for entertaining**

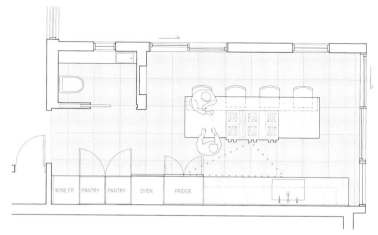

WINE FR. | PANTRY | PANTRY | OVEN | FRIDGE

94 | **Chelsea Kitchen** | London | Johnny Grey Studios

A bright and practical space that fuses color and material to bring natural light floating into this open plan design

108 | **Clovelly Residence** | Sydney | Studio Internationale Pty Limited

A **timeless material** palette includes **honed Carrara marble** and stainless **steel**

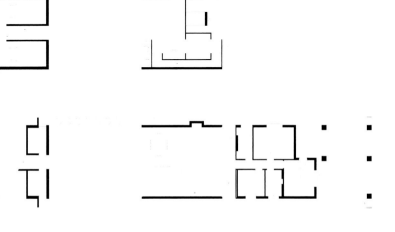

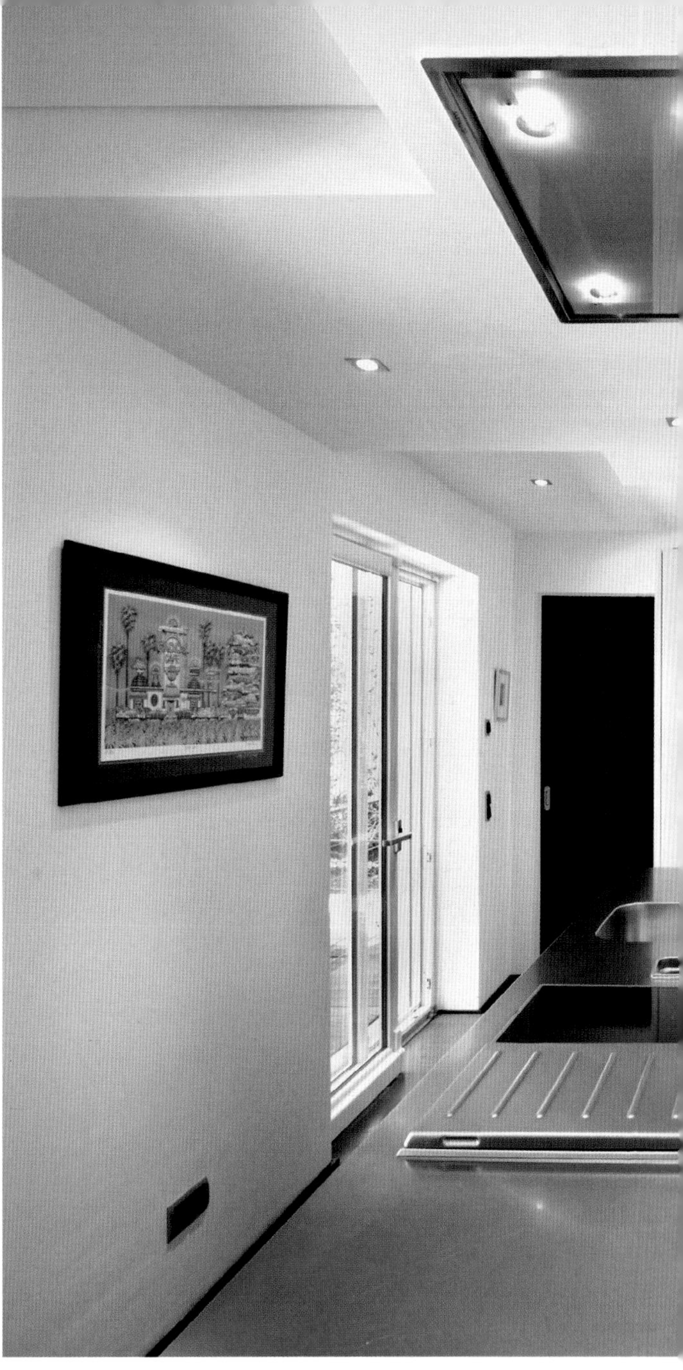

The **countertop** of the **island block** is made from a **single sheet** of steel, the sides are made from **Makassar ebony**

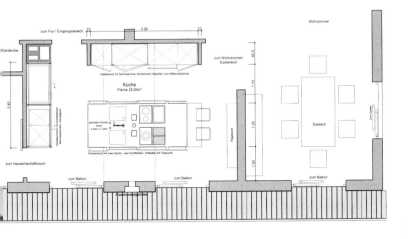

zum Flur / Eingangsbereich

3.26

Wohnzimmer

Garderobe

Garderobenwand mit Spülmaschine, Kühlschrank, Backofen und Kaffeevollautomat

Küche
Fläche 25.00m²

zum Wohnzimmer/
Essbereich

zentraler Küchen-
block
3.48m x 1.25m

Küchenblock mit zwei Spülen, zwei Kochfeldern, Grillplatz und Teppanyaki

Regalwand

Esstisch

2.45

zum Hauswirtschaftsraum

zum Balkon

zum Balkon

zum Balkon

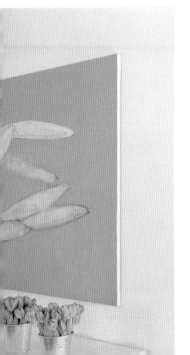

The **finest materials,** a **variety of workspace** and **state-of-the-art** kitchen equipment are **combined** with a **purist touch**

Country House in Westerwald | Dierdorf-Grossmaischeid | Modelsee Architekten

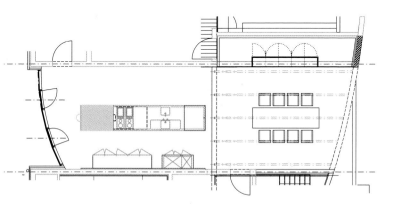

This is a **carefully nested** dwelling on a hillside **organize** between **existing saguaro**

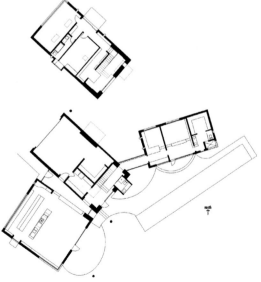

north
↑

Vibrant forms
accentuate the lake view

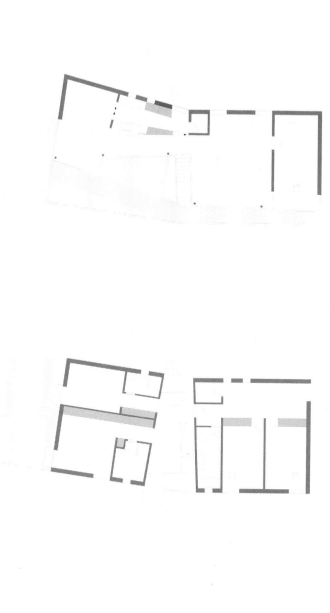

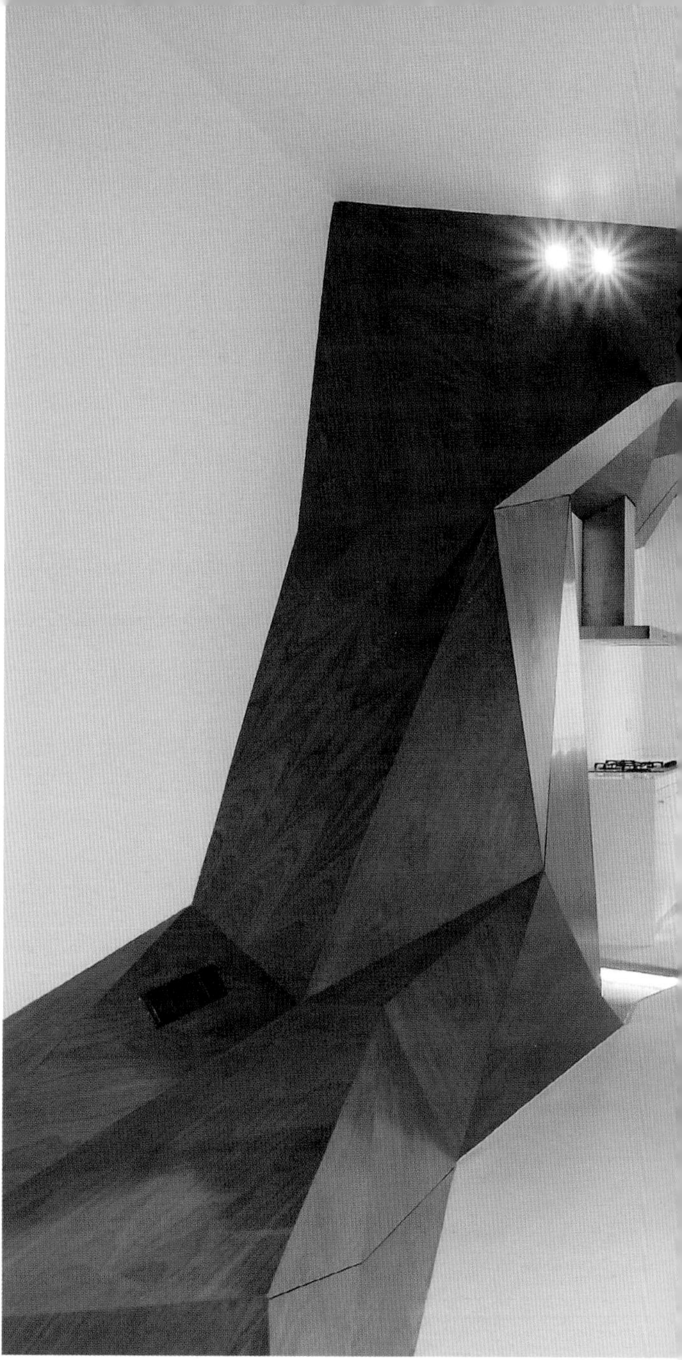

The **cabinet,** in its **movement** around the **white space** of the studio, **becomes** the only **architecture** that is needed

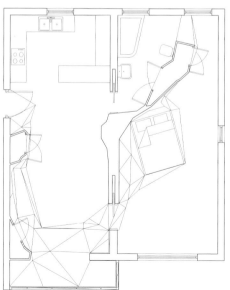

All the **cabinets** are Italian **gray oak,** with grooves **carve** into **each door** to **serve as handle**

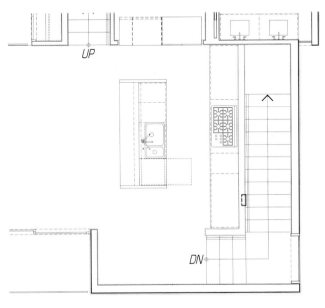

Gammeltorv Walnut Kitchen | Skaelskoer | Knud Kapper Architects

Open-space kitchen
with **hand-built** solid
walnut kitchen **furniture** in
elegant, **classic design**

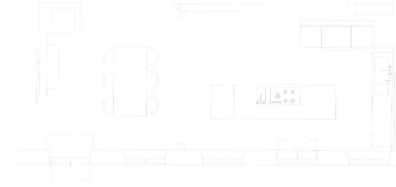

The **cooking equipment** matches **the furniture**

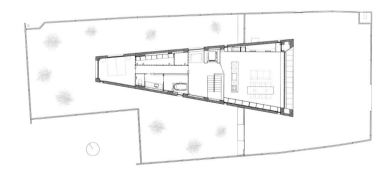

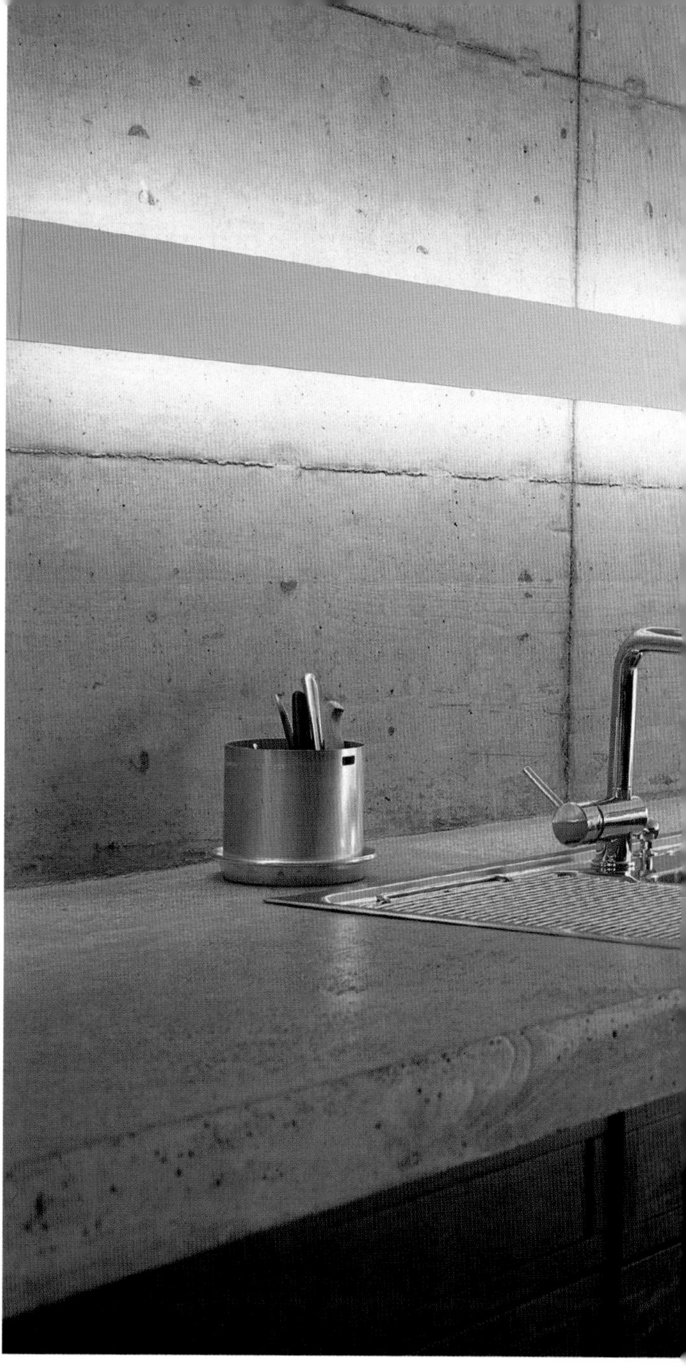

The **particular feature** of this **two-story living** and **dining area** is the preserved **historical living space** with a large open fireplace

Green-HAB is a **building systems prototype** for the rehabilitation of **Baltimore's row houses**

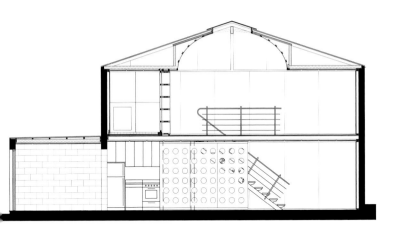

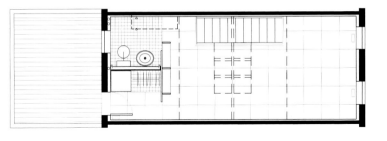

Highgate House | London | Jonathan Clark Architects

The **main idea** here was to produce a **colorful and streamlined** space that give an **illusion of greater** siz

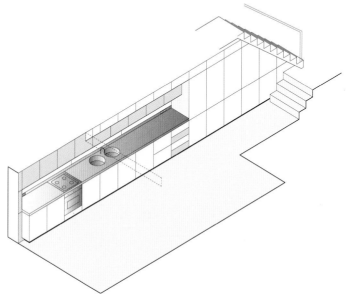

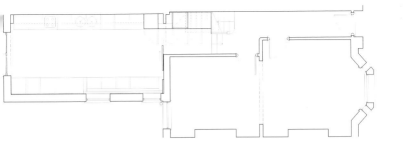

The art of cooking and sharing the results of the experience

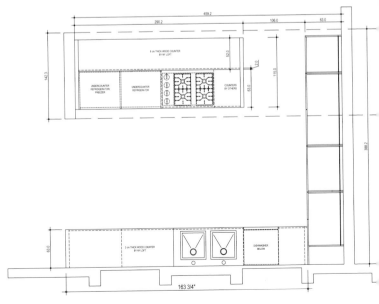

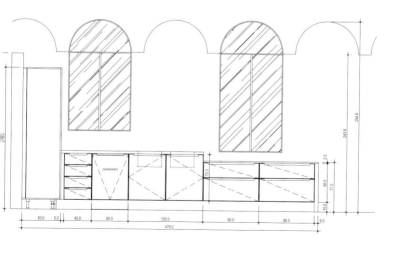

196 | **Kazovsky Renovation** | Los Angeles | Alla Kazovsky Architects

An elegantly functional kitchen, using black oak veneer and reflective surfaces

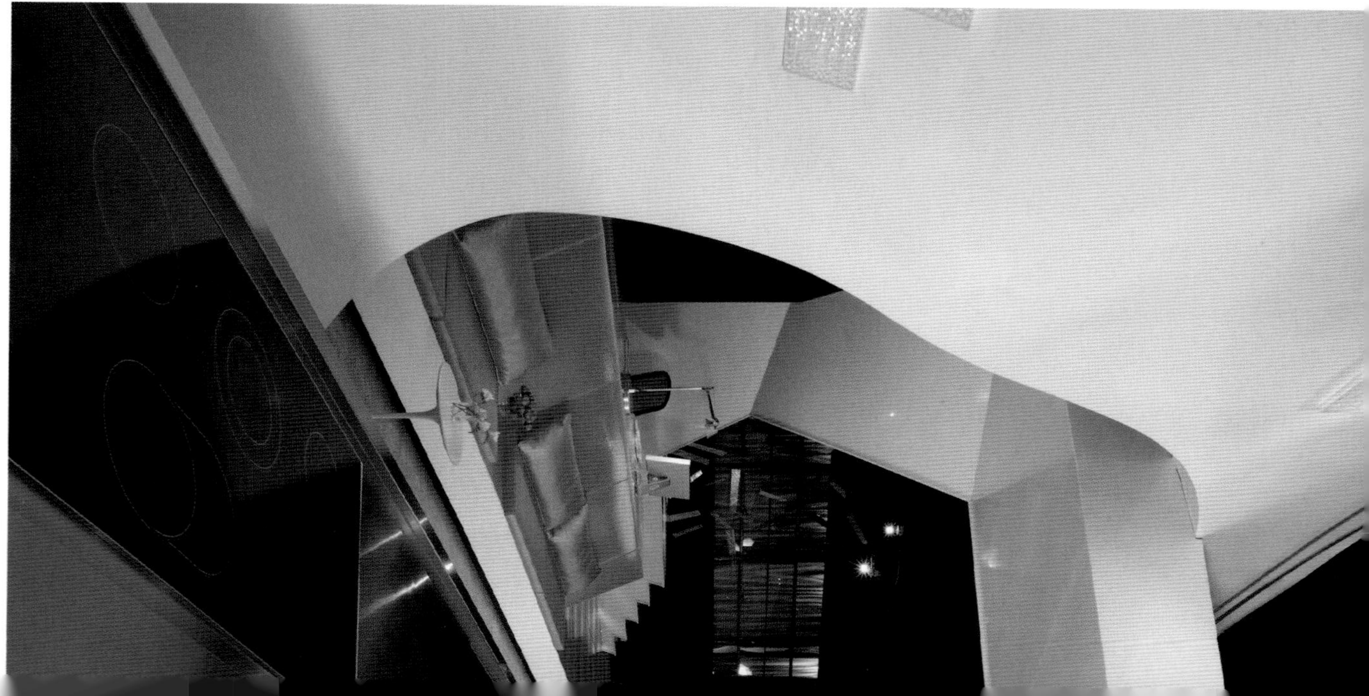

Undulating **curved walls** create
a **womb-like kitchen**

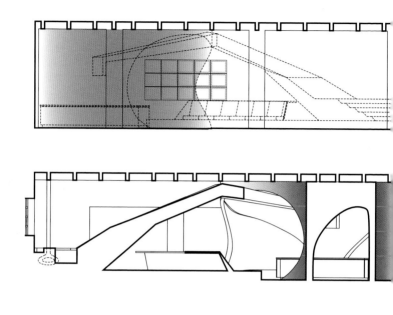

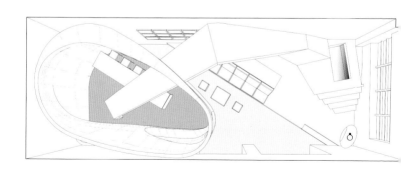

214 | **Lake Street Residence** l San Francisco l CCS Architecture

Showing an **innovative collaboration** that demonstrates how to **satisfy contemporary** lifestyles

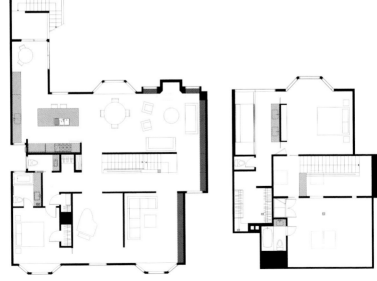

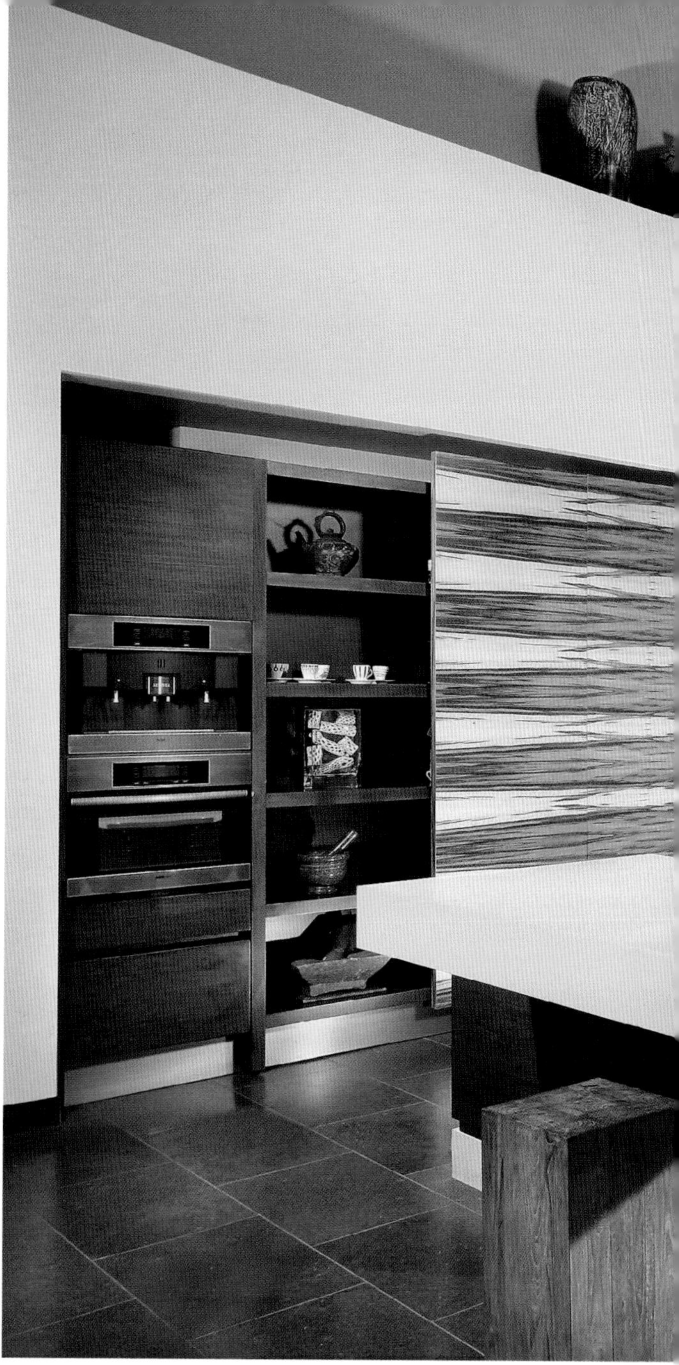

Book-matched walnut, **dark brown** wenge, and **sand-like** Baja Caesarstone create a balanced **modern feeling**

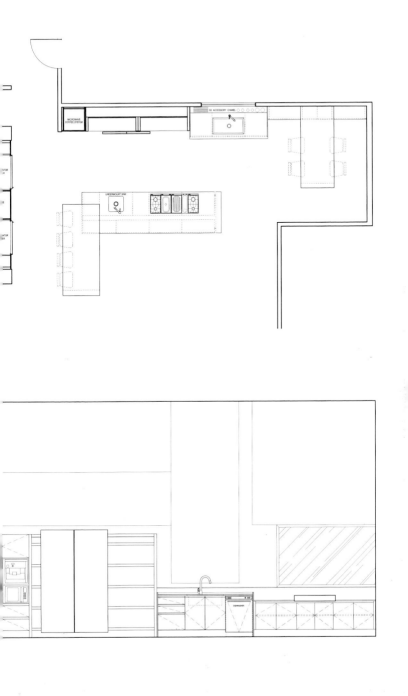

MICROWAVE
COFFEE SYSTEM

02 ACCESSORY CHANNEL

UNDERMOUNT SINK

DISHWASHER

Los Altos Hills Residence | Los Altos Hills | CCS Architecture

The kitchen was **expanded** with access to a **large corner** adding in windows and **including** a 'lounge area' as well

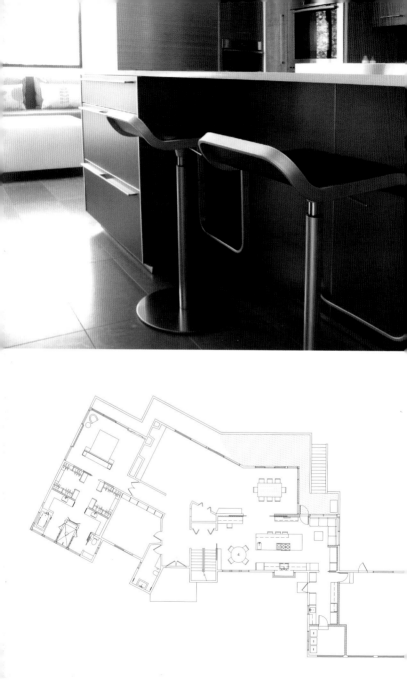

Ultra cool classic **modern** interior of white **Portuguese limeston** throughout

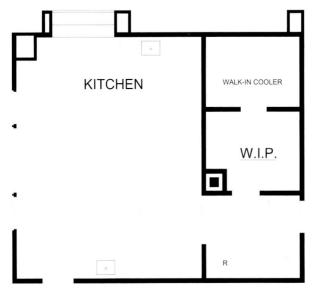

KITCHEN

WALK-IN COOLER

W.I.P.

R

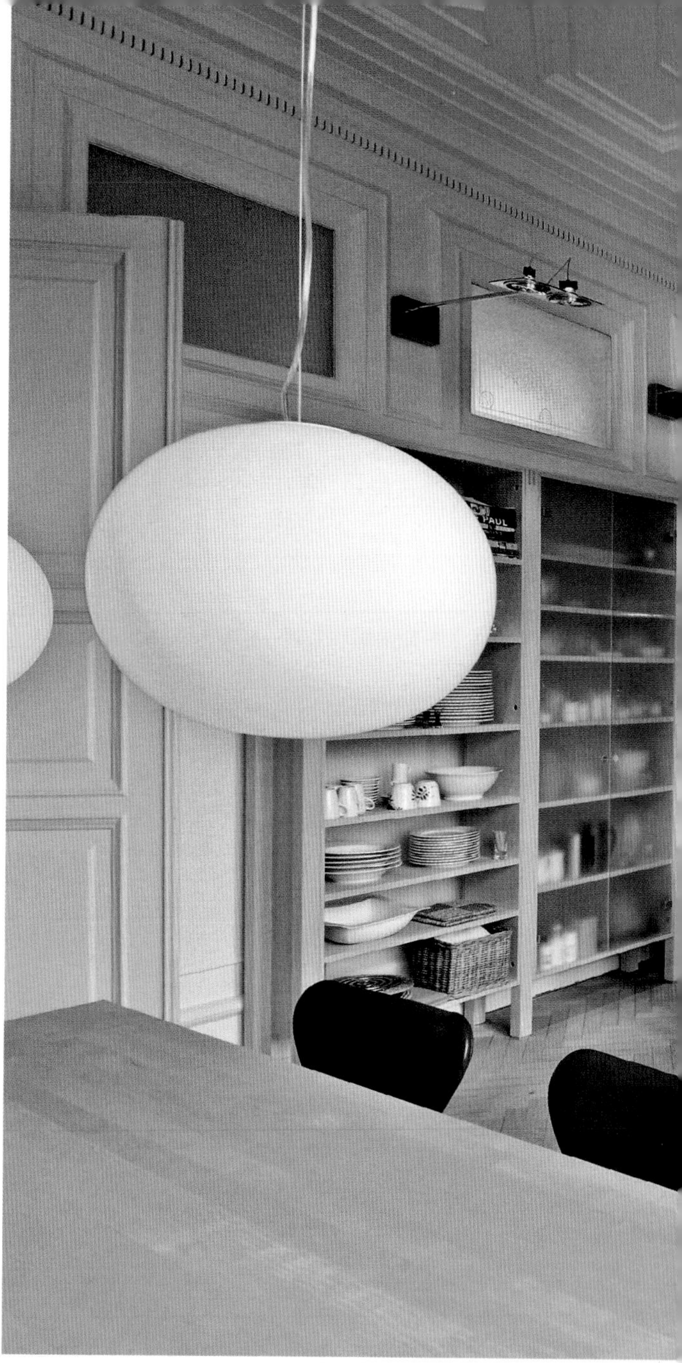

Respecting the **beautiful old panels** this **maple kitchen** was **created to** meet the **owner's professional demands** of cooking

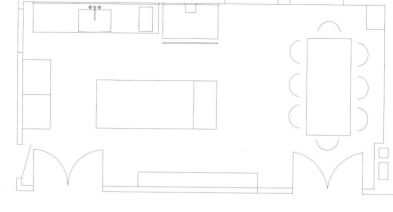

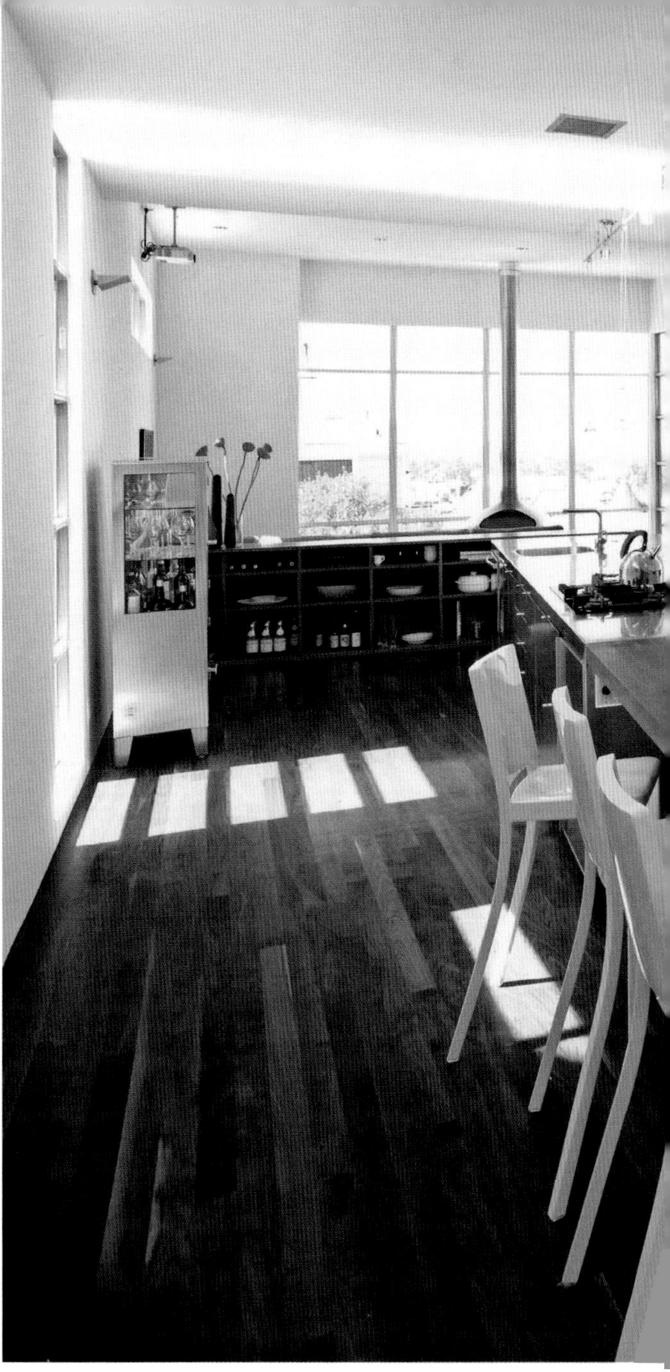

White walls create a **sharp** and **neutral** background for a **balance of walnut** and **stainless steel**

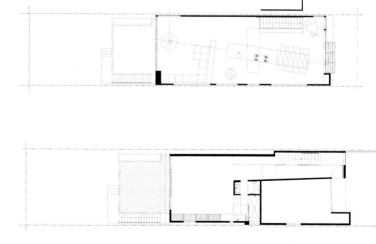

Accentuating the island and **wrapping** seamlessly **down** its side

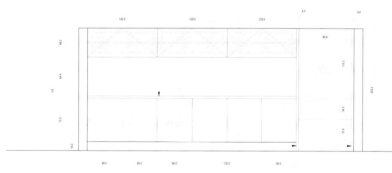

Pedó Eppan House | Eppan | monovolume architecture + design

Kitchen and living room melt into each other

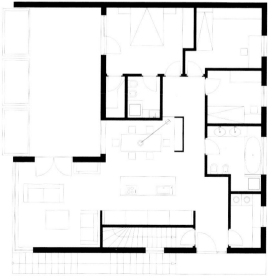

A rectilinear frame **connects the core** to the **library** and **rhymes** with the black and white Corian **kitchen island**

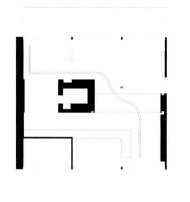
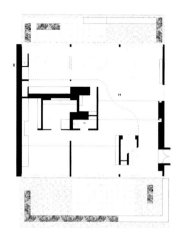

Peaceful neutral colors that
eliminate visual stres

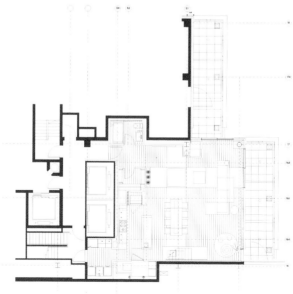

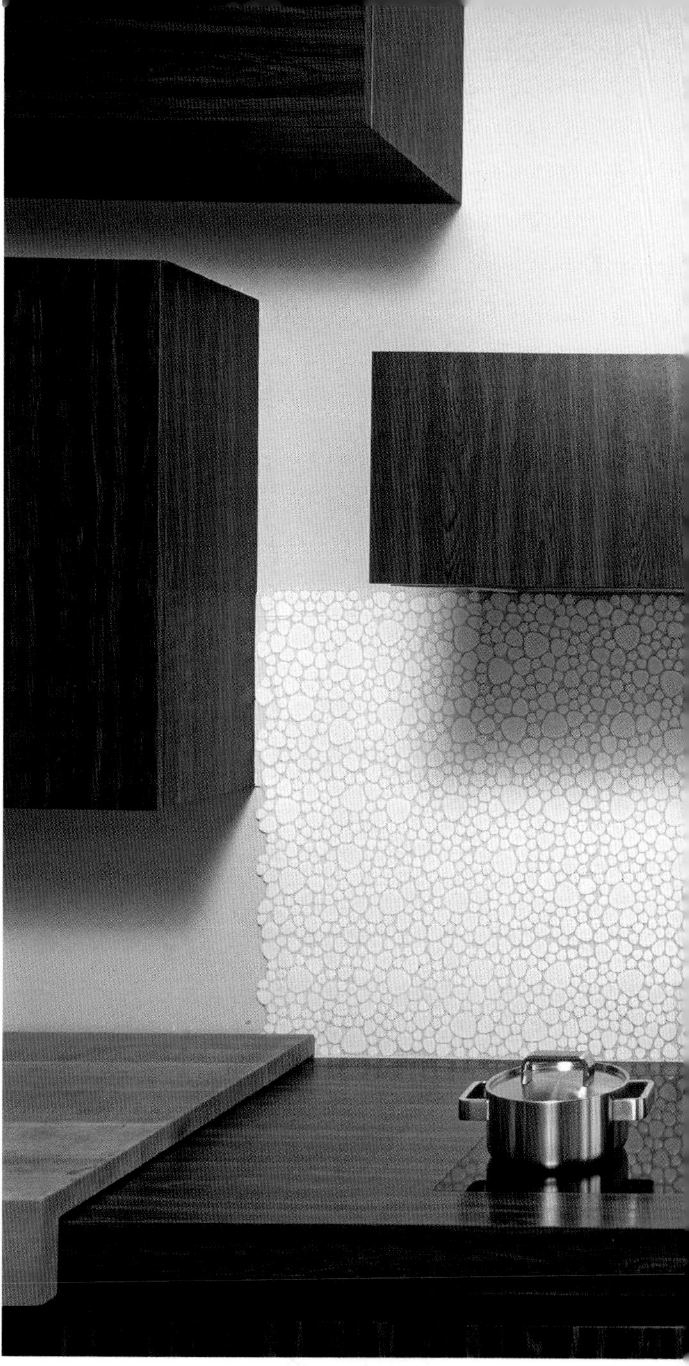

Stylish furniture
in historic shells

Red House | Bragança | Henrique Reinach e Mauricio Mendonça

The **main place** of the house is **the veranda,** which is situated by the pool

Rubin Residence | Bloomfield Hills | McIntosh Poris Associates

The kitchen **blends seamlessly** with the main **floor living area**

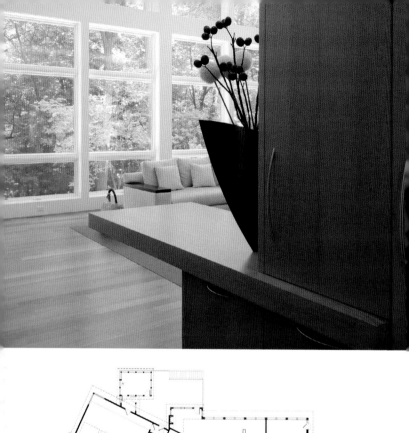

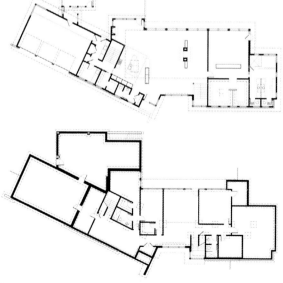

302 | **Space Winding** | Shanghai | MoHen Design International | Hank M. Chao

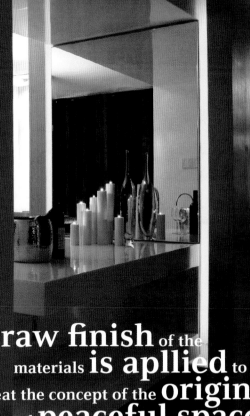

The **raw finish** of the materials **is apllied** to repeat the concept of the **original** and **peaceful space**

St Johns Wood Kitchen | London | Crawford Partnership

This **kitchen connects** the house with **the garden**

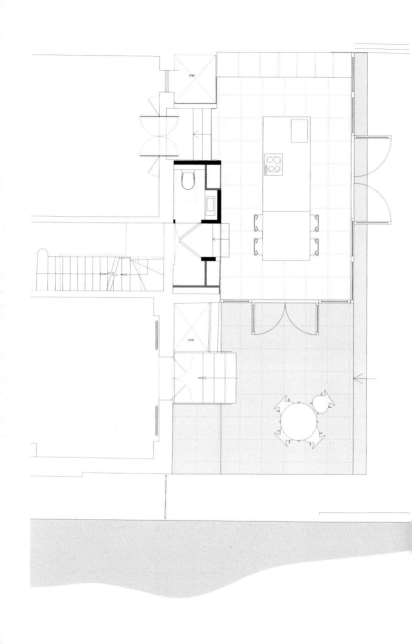

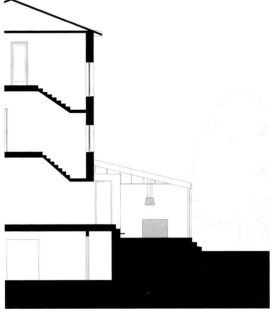

318 | **St Thomas Penthouse** | Toronto | Dubbeldam Design Architects and Kristi Morrison Interiors

A highly functional,
modern kitchen with a clean
industrial aesthetic reveals a
playful side

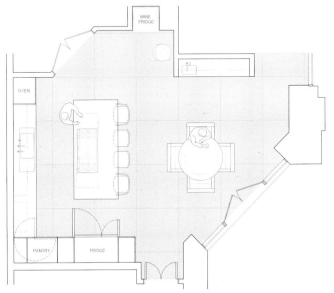

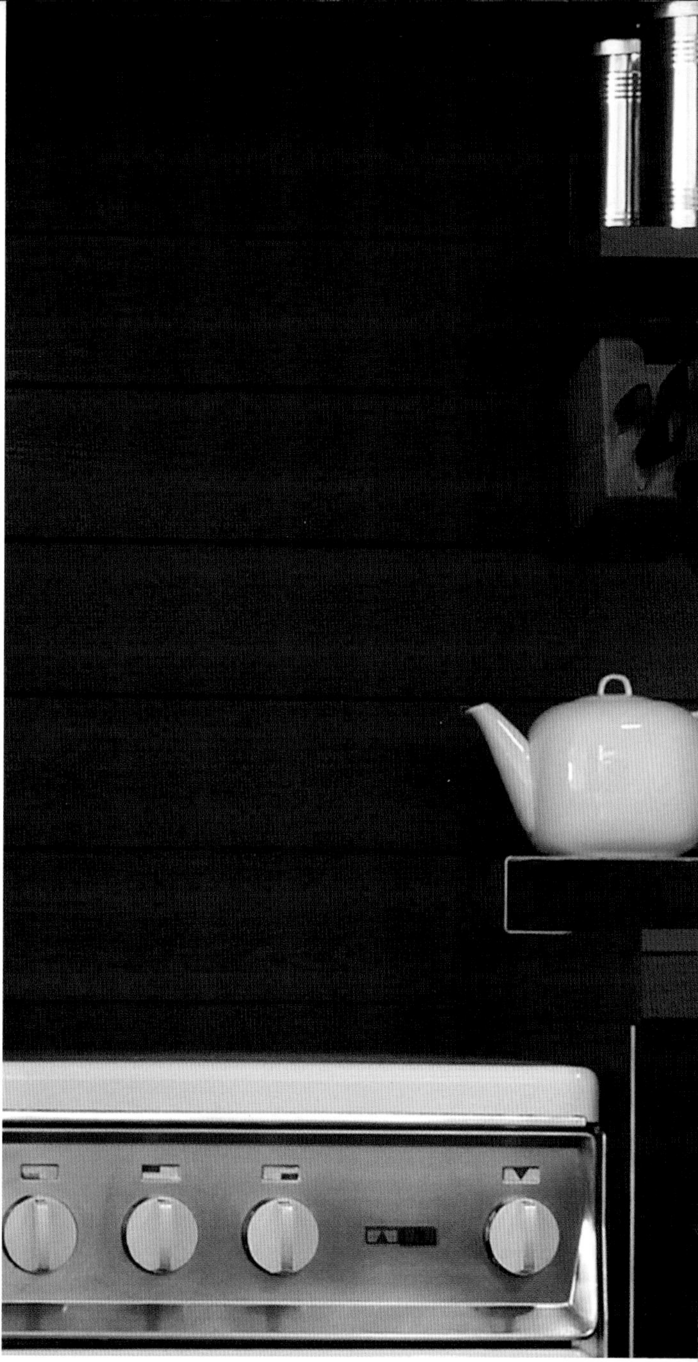

The **cabinets define** the **character** of the **room**

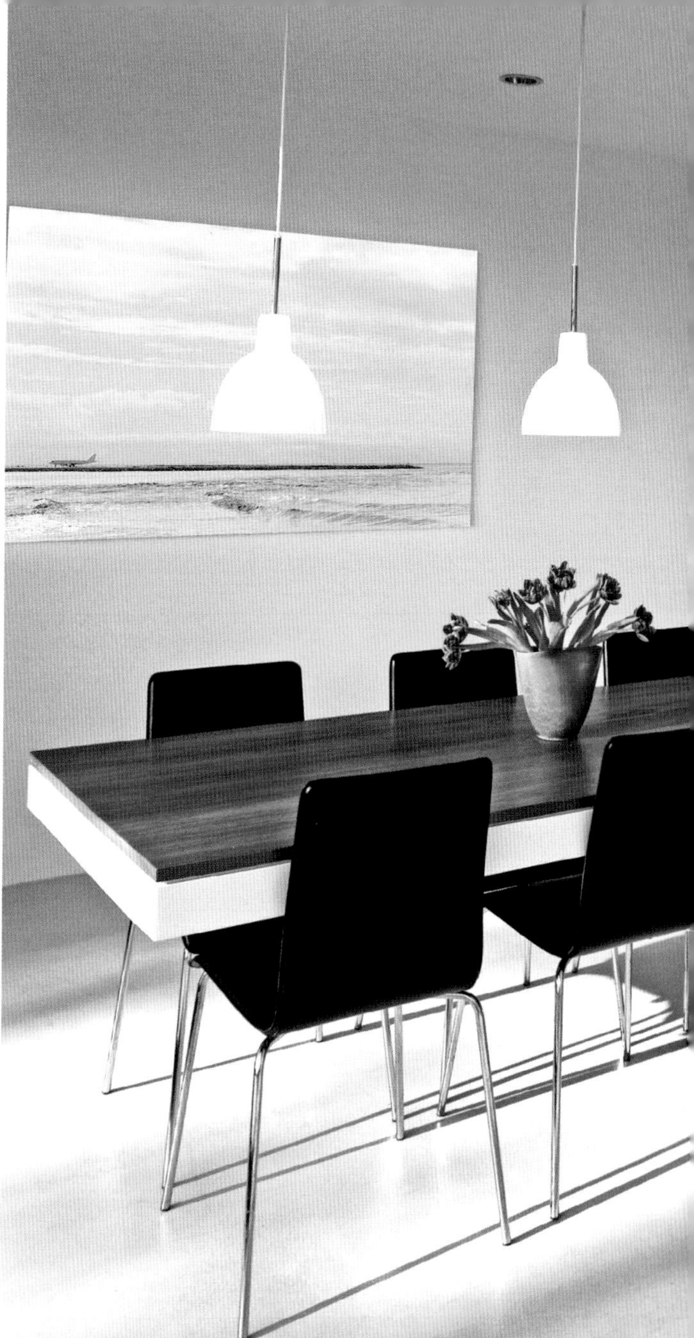

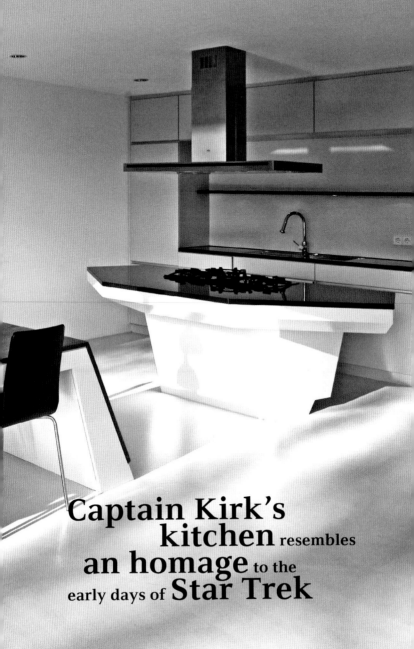

Captain Kirk's kitchen resembles an homage to the early days of Star Trek

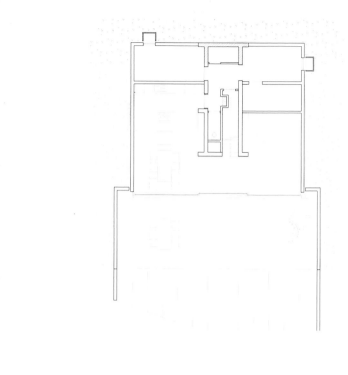

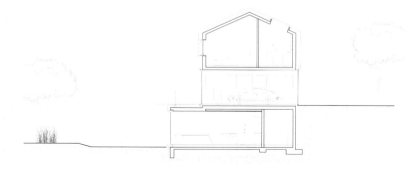

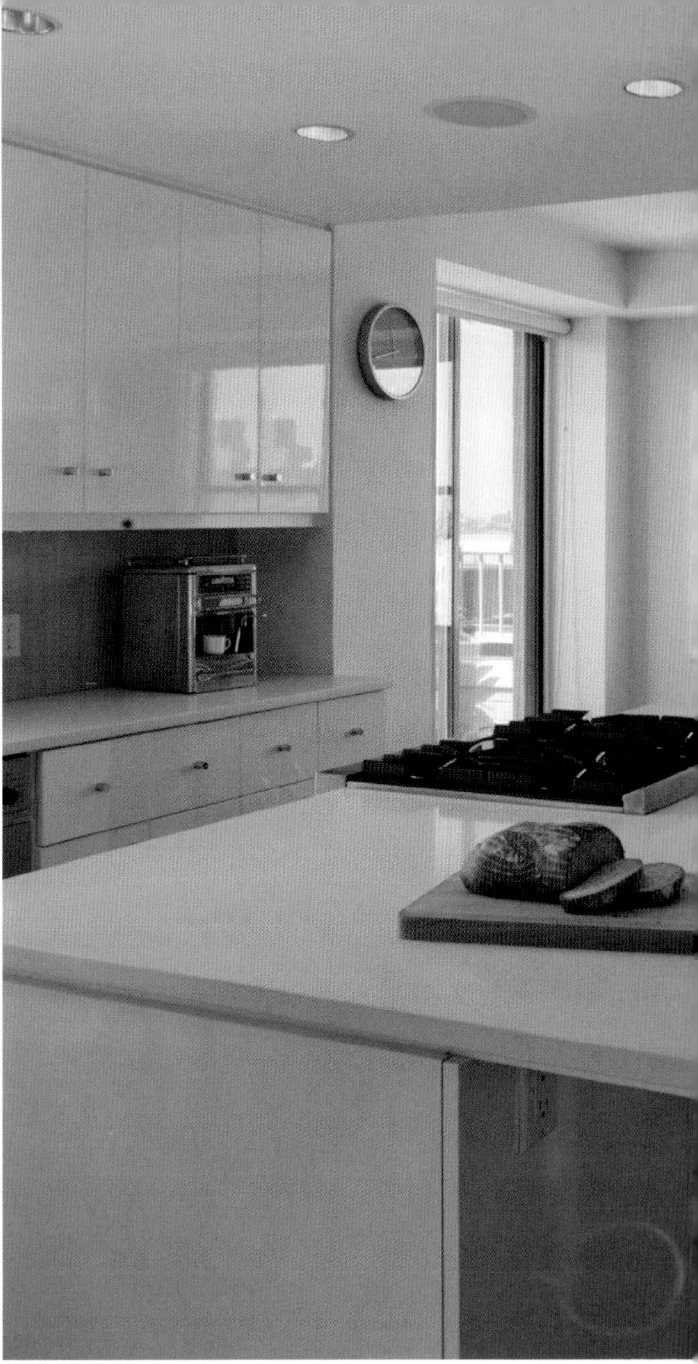

Renovation of 3-bedroom, 3-bathroom apartment for a nightclub owner in the West Village

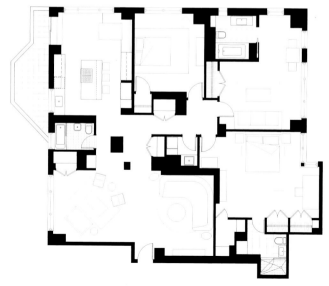

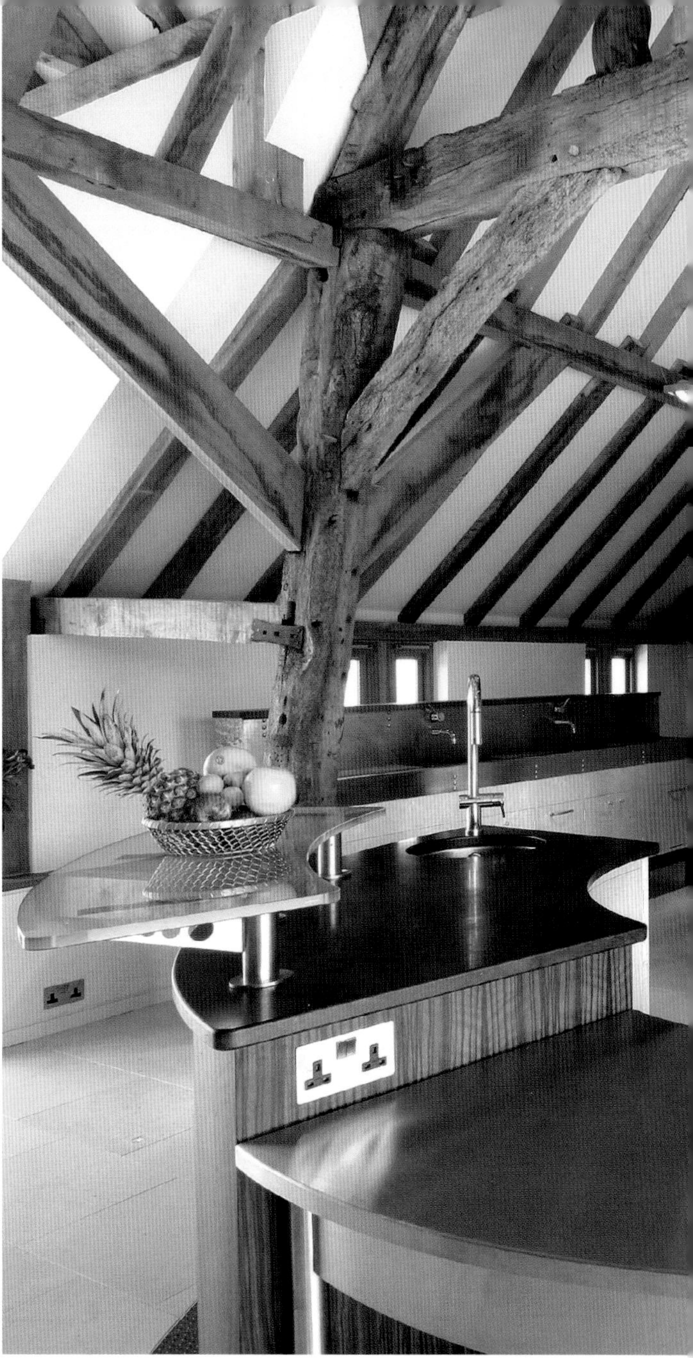

A **unique kitchen** integrated into the **center** of this large **open plan barn** conversion

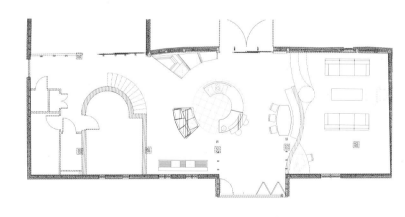

Tilekitchen | undefined | Peter van der Jagt, Erik Jan Kwakkel & Arnout Visser

This project refers to grand-mothers kitchen but is a perfect marriage between inventiveness and craftsmanship

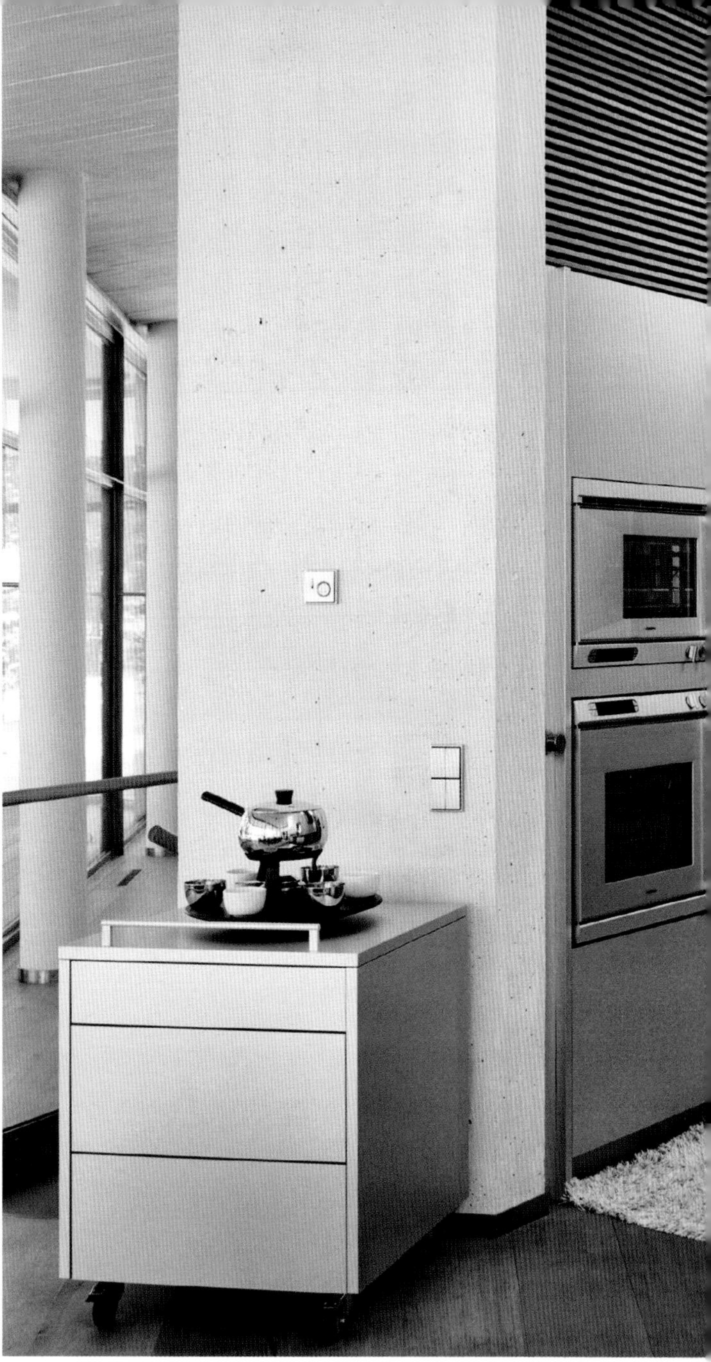

The gleaming light concrete, combined with the texture of the timber formwork, creates a receptive surface for the ample light

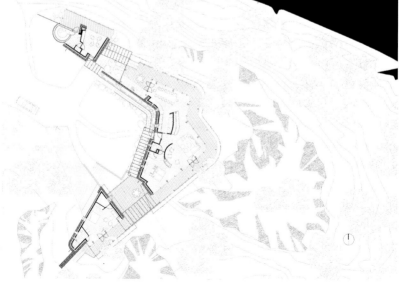

Warehouse Conversion | Melbourne | Greg Gong

The **kitchen bench** is made of dark situ concrete **echoing** the existing **ceiling and columns**

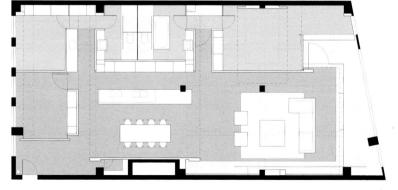

WHITE & STAINLESS STELL | Frankfurt am Main | Andreas Hansel, MORGEN Fine Furniture & Fine Arts

This is a **kitchen-cum-livingroom** with a **Betoplan walnut** unit with stainless **steel worktop**

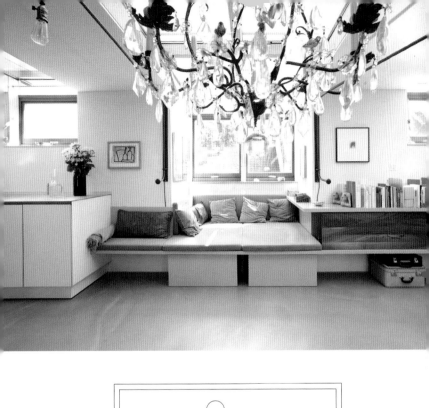

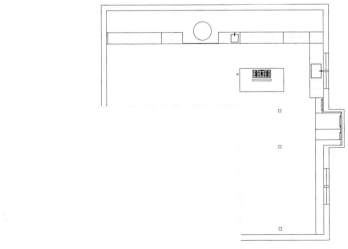

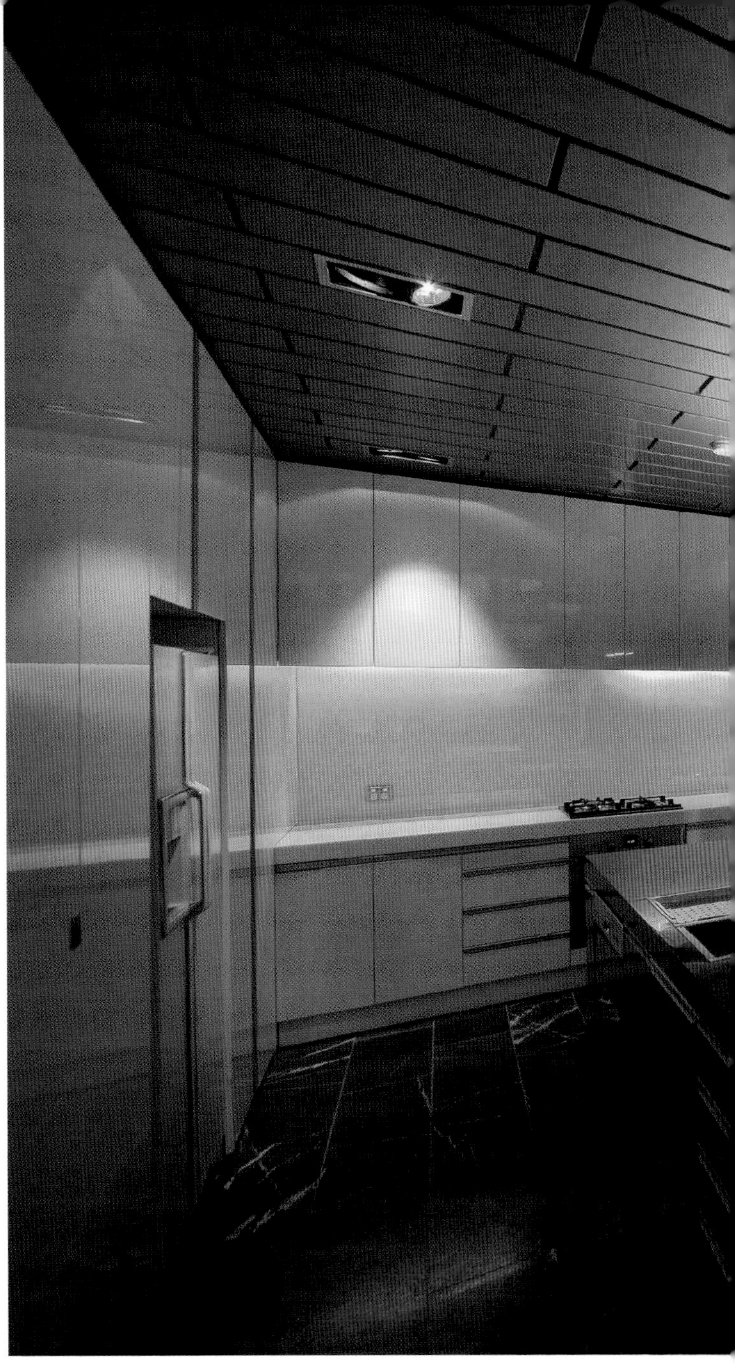

At night the kitchen is designed to entertain and to be the perfect party place

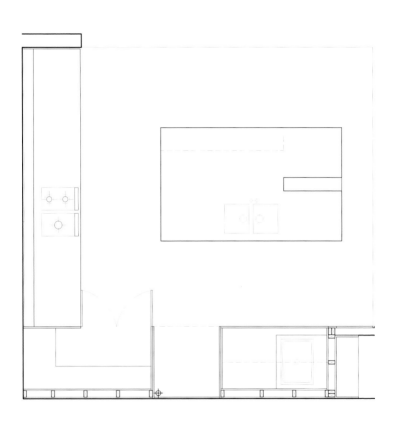

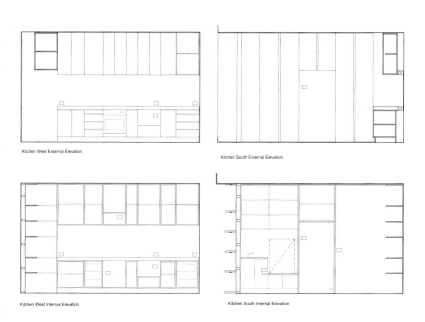

Kitchen West External Elevation

Kitchen South External Elevation

Kitchen West Internal Elevation

Kitchen South Internal Elevation

Architects Index

Picture Credits

Andres Carosio Architekten
  (Katrin Derleth): 140-145
Arban, Tom, Toronto: 318, 319
Art Gray: 204-213
Baldwin, Jan, Narratives: 182-187
Bauman, Kevin, Detroit, MI: 22-25,
  296-299
Chou, Maoder / MoHen Design
  International: 300-307
Constantini, Simon, Brixen: 266-271
Corrnier, Glenn: 234-239
Crocker, Tim, London: 42-49, 308-317
David Franck Photographie,
  Ostfildern: 60-67, 332-339
Dubbeldam, Heather, Toronto:
  320-325
Fern, Susanne: 36-41
Finnotti, Leonardo: 292-295
Fletcher, Joe, San Francisco: 214-221
fotografie andrea dingeldein: 122-131
Gollings, John , Melbourne: 374-379
Griffith, Tim, San Franciso, CA:
  254-259
Insite Photography, Shai Gil: 86-93
James Ewing Photography,
  New York: 340-345
Laignel, Eric, NY: 76-81
Lee, Moon: 282-287
Marquardt, Stefan, Oberursel: 114-121
Meier, Raymond: 54-59
McGolderick, Owne: 240, 241
Holland, Nathan: 222-227
O'Sullivan, Kilian: 272-281
Ott, Thomas: 50-53
Perlmutter, Michael: 368-373
Perrin, Josh , Los Angeles: 196-203
Rubio, Cesar, San Francisco: 78a, 80

Ruppert, Thorsten: 380-389
Salsbery, Eric: 174-181
Jost, Guy: 170-173
Shegedyn, Shania: 395, 396
Timmerman, Bill, Photographer,
  Phoenix, AZ: 132-139, 150-154
Tonn, Dino, Photographer Phoenix,
  AZ: 188-195
Wal, Martin van der: 106-113
Werner, Melissa: 228-233
Winquist, Matt Photographer,
  Phoenix, AZ: 155a
Yano, Tashiyuki
  (Nacasa & Partners Inc.): 162-169
Zirn & Grötsch Photography GmbH:
  82-85

Cover:
Susanne Fern